TIGERS

BY SOPHIE GEISTER-JONES

APEX

WWW.APEXEDITIONS.COM

Copyright © 2022 by Apex Editions, Mendota Heights, MN 55120. All rights reserved. No part of this book may be reproduced or utilized in any form or by any means without written permission from the publisher.

Apex is distributed by North Star Editions:
sales@northstareditions.com | 888-417-0195

Produced for Apex by Red Line Editorial.

Photographs ©: Shutterstock Images, cover, 1, 6–7, 8–9, 12, 13, 16–17, 18–19, 25, 26–27, 29; iStockphoto, 4–5, 10–11, 14–15, 19, 20–21, 22–23, 24

Library of Congress Control Number: 2020952941

ISBN
978-1-63738-035-2 (hardcover)
978-1-63738-071-0 (paperback)
978-1-63738-139-7 (ebook pdf)
978-1-63738-107-6 (hosted ebook)

Printed in the United States of America
Mankato, MN
082021

NOTE TO PARENTS AND EDUCATORS

Apex books are designed to build literacy skills in striving readers. Exciting, high-interest content attracts and holds readers' attention. The text is carefully leveled to allow students to achieve success quickly. Additional features, such as bolded glossary words for difficult terms, help build comprehension.

TABLE OF CONTENTS

CHAPTER 1

HIDDEN HUNTER

A tiger steps out of the trees and into the tall grass. Her large paws muffle her steps. She doesn't make a sound.

A tiger can keep its claws in when it walks.

The tiger watches a boar eat plants. The boar doesn't see her. Her stripes blend in with the grass.

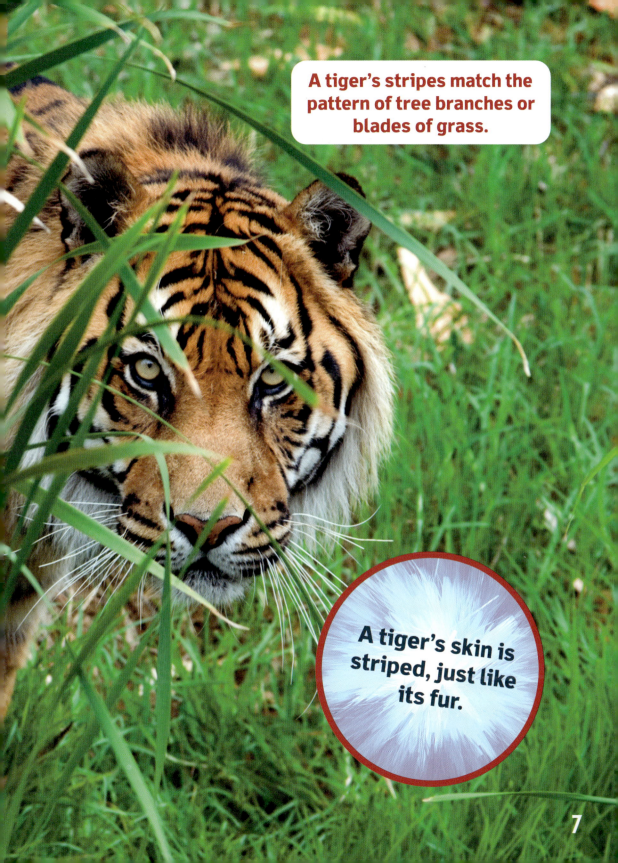

A tiger's stripes match the pattern of tree branches or blades of grass.

A tiger's skin is striped, just like its fur.

For a short time, a tiger can run up to 40 miles per hour (64 km/h).

The tiger creeps silently toward the boar. When she gets close, she **pounces**. She swipes the boar with her claws. Then she bites its throat.

LONG LEGS

A tiger's back legs are longer than its front legs. This helps the tiger jump. It can go nearly 33 feet (10 m) in one leap.

A tiger's claws can be 4 inches (10 cm) long.

CHAPTER 2

LIFE IN THE WILD

Tigers live in Asia. They can survive in many **climates**. They often live in forests or jungles. Some tigers are found on cold mountains. Others live in grasslands or **swamps**.

Tigers that live on cold mountains have thick fur.

Adult tigers usually live alone. But tiger cubs are born small and weak. Their mothers must take care of them.

Tigers can swim as much as 18 miles (29 km) in one day.

A tiger scratches trees to mark its territory. The marks tell other tigers to stay away.

STRIPED SWIMMERS

Tigers often live near water. The large cats are good swimmers. They can catch **prey** in streams or rivers. In hot places, tigers also swim to cool off.

Mother tigers usually have two to four cubs at a time.

Cubs stay with their mother for about two years. She teaches them to hunt and survive. Then, they go live on their own.

Some wild tigers live for 15 years.

CHAPTER 3

STRENGTH AND STRIPES

Tigers have large, strong bodies. Their bodies can be 13 feet (4 m) long. Males tend to be larger than females.

A tiger can weigh up to 660 pounds (299 kg).

Most tigers are orange with dark stripes. But some have white fur and dark stripes. These tigers often have blue eyes.

Most white tigers live in zoos. They are rarely found in the wild.

A tiger's dark stripes can be brown or black.

Every tiger has a different pattern of stripes. No two patterns look the same.

Tigers are powerful **predators**. Their strong bodies make them excellent hunters. They can catch and eat many kinds of animals.

Tigers can leap to catch birds.

A MASSIVE CAT

Tigers are the largest cats in the world. In fact, they are the third largest of all **carnivores**. Only brown bears and polar bears are bigger.

CHAPTER 4

HOW TIGERS HUNT

Tigers are **nocturnal**. They do most of their hunting at night. They mainly eat deer and wild pigs.

A tiger's night vision is six times better than a human's.

A tiger **stalks** its prey. It sneaks close to an animal. Then it pounces. It bites the animal's throat to kill it.

Tigers often hide in tall grass or bushes.

Some tiger teeth are 3 inches (8 cm) long.

TIGER TEETH

Tigers have large **canine teeth**. Tigers use these sharp teeth to tear meat. **Nerves** in the teeth help tigers sense where to bite to kill their prey.

Tigers usually catch prey once per week.

Tigers often hunt big animals. They rarely eat whole animals at one time. Instead, they hide part of their food. They come back later to eat more.

A tiger can eat more than 80 pounds (36 kg) of meat at once.

COMPREHENSION QUESTIONS

Write your answers on a separate piece of paper.

1. Write a sentence describing how tigers hunt their prey.

2. Tigers can live in warm or cold places. Would you rather live somewhere warm or cold?

3. How long do most tiger cubs stay with their mother?

> **A.** 2 years
> **B.** 10 years
> **C.** 15 years

4. Why don't tigers eat whole animals right after catching them?

> **A.** Tigers can't kill animals right away.
> **B.** Tigers don't hunt animals for food.
> **C.** Some animals are too big for tigers to eat at one time.

5. What does **survive** mean in this book?

*They can **survive** in many climates. They often live in forests or jungles.*

    A. to be able to live

    B. to be afraid to live

    C. to not be found somewhere

6. What does **muffle** mean in this book?

*Her large paws **muffle** her steps. She doesn't make a sound.*

    A. to make something louder

    B. to make something quieter

    C. to make something melt

Answer key on page 32.

GLOSSARY

canine teeth
Large, pointed teeth near the front of an animal's mouth.

carnivores
Animals that eat meat.

climates
The usual weather in certain areas.

nerves
Long, thin fibers that carry information between the brain and other parts of the body.

nocturnal
Awake and active at night.

pounces
Jumps on something to catch it.

predators
Animals that hunt and eat other animals.

prey
An animal that is hunted and eaten by another animal.

stalks
Slowly and quietly sneaks toward something.

swamps
Areas of low land covered in water, often with many plants.

TO LEARN MORE

BOOKS

Dickmann, Nancy. *Bengal Tigers*. Tucson: Brown Bear Books, 2019.

Janes, Patricia. *Tigers*. New York: Scholastic, 2018.

Sommer, Nathan. *Siberian Tiger vs. Brown Bear*. Minneapolis: Bellwether Media, 2021.

ONLINE RESOURCES

Visit **www.apexeditions.com** to find links and resources related to this title.

ABOUT THE AUTHOR

Sophie Geister-Jones lives in Saint Paul, Minnesota. She loves reading. She and her brothers have a book club.

INDEX

Answer Key:
1. Answers will vary; **2.** Answers will vary; **3.** A; **4.** C; **5.** A; **6.** B